Window on Love

The Ultimate Guide to Sexual Fulfillment

Dr LASSE HESSEL

CRAWFORD HOUSE PRESS

BATHURST

A CHP Production

Produced and published by
Crawford House Press International Pty Ltd
P.O. Box 1484
Bathurst NSW 2795 Australia

Distributed by Publishers Group West

ISBN   1 86333 060 7

Printed in Hong Kong by Colorcraft Ltd

10 9 8 7 6 5 4 3 2 1

Window on Love

The Ultimate Guide to Sexual Fulfillment

Contents

Preface

I wish to thank all the couples who participated in the many scans that formed the basis of this book.

It has been a pioneering task that has demanded both courage and an urge to explore. I appreciate that it has taken much more time than I initially told the couples. There was also some awkwardness in certain cases, so not all couples could be scanned in every position.

Most of the people who were tested needed two to four test days before the actual video recording could start. Youngsters became familiar with the set-up quite easily, but the more mature couples had to come back several times before performing 'natural sexual intercourse'. But when the couples were left alone doing their own scanning, they all claimed they had been able to make love in a normal way. As a whole, the pregnant women also achieved satisfactory results.

Not all couples could perform each of the ten positions, as some had trouble keeping the ultrasound scanner in the right position during intercourse.

A new method, which shows what occurs inside the woman during intercourse, has now been proven, but of course the sum of knowledge and results is incomplete. This is the beginning of a new research field in which studies will no doubt be carried out worldwide. Within the next few years, this research will provide us with new important knowledge about the anatomy and physiology of sexual intercourse.

The most important thing for an author is, of course, that the readers can benefit from his or her book, so I feel I must recount a wonderful story from a letter I received from a couple aged 82 and 72 years. In their letter they state: "Even though we are now respectively 82 and 72 years old and still perform sexual activity, we had never been able to stimulate the so-called G-spot until now. It has increased our sexual pleasure and activity so much that we decided to give the book to both our children and grandchildren!"

I hope this shows that both young and old can benefit and receive joy from this new basic knowledge.

Foreword

This is a book on heterosexual intercourse. Sexuality is a much discussed theme. There are many books on sex education for children and young people. For adults, there are books on how to become a better lover.

Window on Love is not specifically meant for youths or adults alone. It provides information on sexual intercourse for young and old, for the experienced and inexperienced, and it explains which positions give the best stimulation.

I, for one, am delighted with *Window on Love*. As a sexological therapist, I have noticed more than once that many people really don't know much about intercourse. They 'do it' together, yes – but how? Very often it is done only one way – man on top, woman under – even though most women get very little sexual stimulation out of it. This book shows many other ways of having sexual intercourse. The descriptions are accompanied by a full explanation of the spots which are stimulated most in each of the various positions, so every woman and every man can discover the way in which she or he is best satisfied.

The information in this book is unusual in that scanning techniques have been used. Sexual intercourse can be 'looked at' in the same way an unborn child can be shown during pregnancy, by means of sonic waves. Thanks to these scanning techniques we have a better understanding of sexual intercourse – including sex during pregnancy.

This book will enable men and women to get more pleasure from sex, as it enhances knowledge of how intercourse takes place inside the women. It is not meant to sing the praises of sexual intercourse as the only way to make love – some people might not like having intercourse at all! Maybe this book will provide such people with information through which they will come to enjoy sex. Sexual intercourse is only one way of making love; other ways are neither worse nor better. But if you do have intercourse, this book will be very useful for you and your partner.

Willeke Bezemer
Psychologist and Sexologist

Introduction

This book examines the act of sex from a new perspective. It uses special ultrasound scanning techniques, among others, to view the human sexual act inside the body of a woman while intercourse is actually taking place. This research has produced accurate knowledge of how to achieve the best stimulation of the body's erogenous zones. These zones are the areas on the human body which are susceptible to sexual stimulation, and are described in detail later.

The results of this study are intended to provide a guide to lovemaking, and address beginners as well as more experienced couples of all ages.

This is not an advanced and scholarly presentation of anatomical and physiological phenomena, but a practical handbook to be followed word by word, drawing by drawing and page by page. It aims to present its contents in an educational and unsensational format, factually showing what happens internally during lovemaking, and thus hopes to contribute to a better and more fulfilling love life.

It makes sense for both you and your partner to try to understand and achieve the very best of this aspect of life so that it becomes as varied, exciting, mutually pleasurable and, most importantly, as natural as possible.

For the first time, scanning techniques have been employed to research lovemaking as it occurs. This work offers remarkable information on aspects of sexual intercourse which have never been seen before, plus new knowledge about the movement and interaction of the vagina, uterus and penis during intercourse.

Although there are countless different positions for making love, the ten particular examples shown in this book are presented as some of the most common options used, with many variations on each being perfectly normal. Photographs of the results of scanning give the reader an insight into the relative positions of the vagina and penis during intercourse, and show how the erogenous zones can best be stimulated.

It is important to remember that everyone is built differently; no two individuals are the same. This book gives general guidelines – you should only use the drawings as inspiration, and not take them too literally.

If you and your partner can find just one satisfying new position, then the aim of the book has been fulfilled.

It is assumed that the readers of this book are aware of the absolute necessity of taking the precaution of using a condom, either a male or a female one, to protect themselves against sexually transmitted diseases such as AIDS if they are having sexual relations with a person whose long-term sexual history is unknown.

Scanning

In recent years it has been possible to take the most remarkable pictures of the inside of the human body. We have seen how blood flows within our veins, how cholesterol causes arteriosclerosis, and many other secrets. We have been able to watch the heart pumping, and to follow the marvels of the digestive process through the stomach and intestines. Literally speaking, no part of the human body has been left hidden. We have obtained fascinating insights into the internal organs of the body and how they function.

For the first time, ultrasound scanning techniques make it possible to obtain an insight into how the internal sexual organs of the female are influenced, together with the male's penis, during sexual intercourse. Pictures from the scan are recorded during lovemaking in different positions, so it is possible both to study the whole sequence, and also to freeze-frame and examine the results on a time basis. For instance, the position of the penis in the vagina and the movements of the cervix and uterus are shown by this technique.

The results are simply astonishing. The walls of the vagina are completely passive during intercourse, apart from a distinct indentation which occurs at a place corresponding to the base of the bladder. Furthermore, it is amazing to observe that the entire uterus can move vigorously up and down within the female pelvis during intercourse.

There has been another remarkable observation from the ultrasound scanning during intercourse. In women who have given birth, and consequently have a more elastic vagina, the penis tends to touch the front wall of the vagina near the base of the bladder, where the female G-spot is normally situated (see page 18). In women who have not given birth, the penis tends to reach as far as the bottom of the vagina, and comes close to the cervix, but does not stimulate the G-spot.

This difference may explain why many women do not experience orgasm until their late twenties or even their thirties, after having given birth.

In order to allow the penis head, or glans, to stimulate the area where the G-spot is situated, near the base of the bladder, it is a good idea for women who are not pregnant to empty their bladder before lovemaking (see Scan 1).

During the scanning investigations of intercourse, it was felt very important to find out what occurred inside the body of a pregnant female in relation to her unborn baby. This is a little-understood area of medical knowledge, and the results are very interesting.

Highlighted photographs of scans are shown here, and the five most important features have been marked for clarity. The test subject was five months pregnant.

Scan 1 shows how a full bladder protects the foetus against thrusts from the penis by forming a 'water buffer' between the penis and uterus. (Compare with the position on page 60.) This means the foetus remains steady and does not move up and down during intercourse.

Scan 2 shows that the foetus is also protected when the bladder is only half full.

Scan 3, however, shows that if the woman's

a. Vagina b. Penis c. Bladder d. Placenta e. Foetus

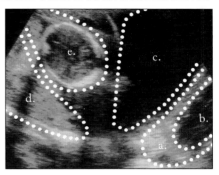

1. Full bladder

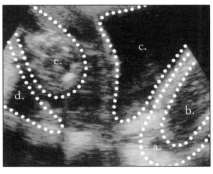

2. Half full bladder

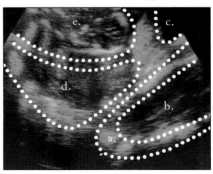

3. Empty bladder

bladder is empty, the 'water buffer' is no longer there. The penis hits the edge of the placenta, and the foetus bobs up and down during intercourse. We do not know whether having intercourse with an empty bladder increases the risk of losing the baby, but it is a fact that miscarriage can be caused by bleeding from the placenta.

The technique used to produce the photographs involves using a special scanner which produces very fast, harmless sound waves. These resonate in different ways when passing through air, tissue and internal organs, according to the composition of the material through which they pass. The black areas on the photographs appear because they do not exhibit resonance; that is, the material does not reflect the sound. The white areas exhibit strong resonance, which means strong reflection of sound; in other words, a poor penetration of the sound waves shows up on the scan. When, for example, the urinary bladder is black on the photo, it is because urine does not reflect sound.

DRAWINGS FROM THE SCAN

The illustrations on page 15 are drawn from the scans, and show different stages during intercourse. The people who were tested were voluntary medical student couples. These new scientific discoveries are, of course, not reserved solely for the medical profession, and are shown here for the first time to non-medical people.

The purpose of this book is to show, in the most graphic, unsensational and comprehensive way, how different positions during intercourse can stimulate those zones identified during the scanning investigations.

By studying these pictures and following the ten typical intercourse positions shown at the end of the book, you and your partner can together find out how to achieve the highest degree of pleasure, reaching climax and satisfaction. But do not forget it takes practice, full commitment and concentration from both before you can succeed.

The explanation of the ten intercourse positions is concluded with a table on page 64: 'Summary of Positions'. Using this table, it is easy to see how the clitoris, G-spot, glans and so on, which are discussed later, are best stimulated, and the positions securing the best and most satisfactory interaction between male and female.

Diagram 1. Remember to allow the penis to gently stimulate the clitoris area on its way into the vagina.

Diagram 2. When inside the vagina, the male should not immediately penetrate fully, but stop and make small movements with his penis to ensure the penis head stimulates the G-spot area.

Diagram 3. When the penis is all the way into the vagina, the male must not forget to stimulate the clitoris area with the root of his penis.

Diagram 4. Withdraw very slowly from the female, and make sure the penis again stimulates the G-spot as much as possible. This can be achieved if both partners rotate their pelvises to find the most stimulating positions.

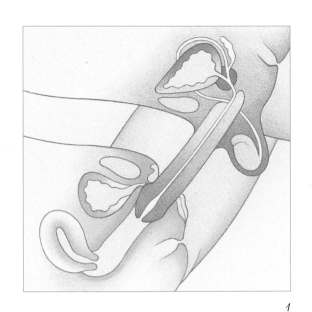

1

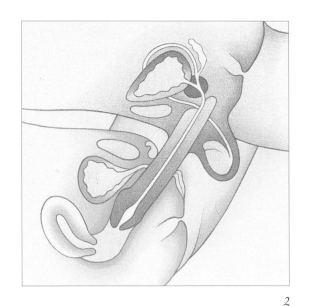

2

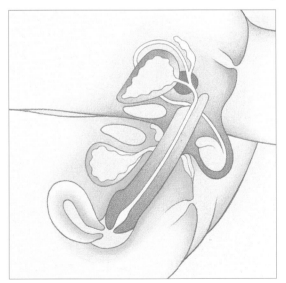

3

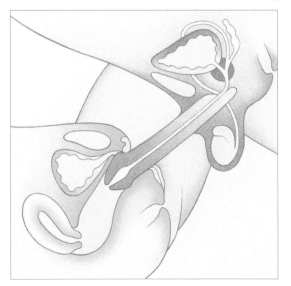

4

15

Anatomy

General drawings of the genitals of men and women are shown on the following pages. There is, of course, no one person who looks precisely like this. This is because the different internal organs in human beings move in relation to each other, and no two human beings are built completely alike. We all know some people have big noses, others have small ones, and some people are tall and others short. The same is also true about the genitals. The length of the penis varies from 8 to 24 cm (3 to 9½ inches) when erect. The vagina usually varies less, in that it is about 12 to 16 cm deep (4½ to 6½ inches).

All the same, it is most important not to worry about whether the sizes of the penis and the vagina are compatible, partly because the vagina is so extremely variable, and partly because the size of the penis has absolutely no significance for the woman as far as achieving orgasm is concerned.

The schematic drawings should not, therefore, be taken too literally, and you are not at all abnormal if your anatomy falls outside what is depicted. For example, the illustrated G-spot positions, discussed later, can vary significantly, and for some women the spot does not exist at all. A woman can still reach orgasm if she has no G-spot.

In addition, the position, shape and size of the clitoris can vary considerably. The clitoris can be big or small, and can either be situated down at the opening of the front of the vagina, or higher up behind the mons, or genital hair area. This point is also discussed later.

ANATOMY OF THE VAGINA AND ASSOCIATED SURROUNDING ORGANS

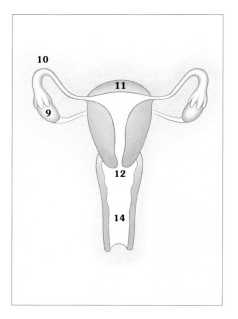 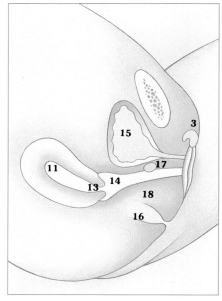 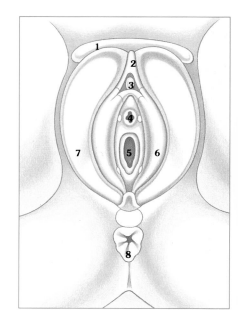

1. Mons pubis.
2. Clitoris body: similar to the man's penis.
3. Clitoris head: similar to the man's glans.
4. Opening of the urethra.
5. Entrance to the vagina.
6. Labia minores.
7. Labia majores.

8. Anus.
9. Ovary.
10. Uterine (Fallopian) tube.
11. Cavity of the uterus.
12. Cervix.
13. Cavity of the cervix.
14. Cavity of the vagina.

15. Urinary bladder.
16. Anal canal.
17. G-spot: approximate location (see page 12).
18. Second G-spot: approximate location (see page 12).

ANATOMY OF THE PENIS AND ASSOCIATED SURROUNDING ORGANS

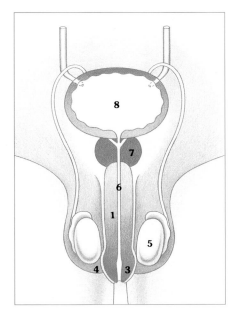 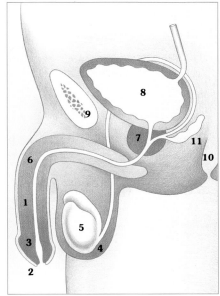 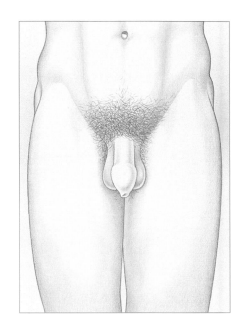

1. *Penis: contains special veins, called corpus cavernosum penis. When the blood is blocked here the penis swells up and becomes thick and hard.*
2. *Foreskin: if present, covers the penis (a number of males are circumcised).*
3. *Glans: the end, or head, of the penis, which is the most sensitive part.*
4. *Scrotum: covers the testicles.*
5. *Testicles: produce sperm.*
6. *Urethra: the duct for both urine and sperm.*
7. *Prostate gland: produces a special alkaline secretion that neutralises the acid in the vagina so the sperm can survive until it reaches the uterus.*
8. *Urinary bladder.*
9. *Pubic bone.*
10. *Anal canal.*
11. *G-spot: approximate location (see page 22)*

General Comments

Satisfactory lovemaking depends on the partners in a couple choosing a position which gives them both the best physical stimulation. The only people who can decide whether they have chosen the right position are those making love.

Just as there are innumerable different body types, there is an almost indefinite number of variations of position and stimulation which will result in satisfactory lovemaking.

A word of warning about the widespread attitude – especially prevalent among young people – that the number and variety of positions plays a part in successful lovemaking. On the contrary, couples end up using a limited number of positions after early experimentation, and normally have neither the need nor the desire to try new sexual acrobatics each time they make love.

However, once in a while and perhaps on special occasions, experimenting with positions different from those normally used during lovemaking can lead to new sensations and experiences for everyone, including established couples.

The descriptions on the following pages are meant to be both a practical guide for couples who have not yet found a full repertoire of positions, as well as a guide for those who want to understand previously unknown aspects of their bodies.

Most of the suggestions mentioned are based on the ultrasound scanning experiments which, for the first time, make it possible to study what happens inside the woman's pelvis during intercourse. By referring to pictures taken during scanning, we are able to reveal not only the position of the penis, but also the reaction of the vagina and uterus during these physically intense moments.

In the positions shown towards the end of the book, it can be seen that the penis can be directed into different positions, and thus stimulate various sensitive areas of the vagina and other sexual organs of the female. A man can easily feel which position stimulates him most. It is common for him to want to change position once or more during lovemaking, either to seek maximum stimulation and reach climax more swiftly, or to minimise stimulation so that his climax can be delayed until the woman reaches her orgasm.

Although a lot of scientific research has been carried out to discover what causes orgasm or

climax, there is no total agreement. In most men it occurs primarily when the area of the glans is stimulated, but for some it is just as important, or perhaps even more so, to stimulate all of the penis in order to reach climax.

Many sexologists consider that the female orgasm develops from the clitoris, and spreads from there to the vagina and pelvis. However, other sexologists believe German gynaecologist, Dr Grafenberg, is correct in his description of the so-called G-spot, from which a vaginal orgasm can originate. The truth is probably that both theories are right; some women achieve orgasm from the clitoris, others have a vaginal orgasm, and perhaps the majority have a combination of the two.

The G-spot is thought to be a small pea-sized area of blood vessels, glands and sensitive nerve endings situated halfway up the front of the vagina, just behind the pubis (see page 18). In some women it is situated near the entrance of the vagina, while in others it may be higher up the front wall. A woman can try to identify the actual position of her G-spot by inserting her finger 2 to 5 cm (about 1 to 2 inches) up her vagina and massaging this area. If this is done for too long or too forcefully it may cause discomfort or even pain. The area of the G-spot is usually sensitive just after orgasm – but not as sensitive as the clitoris. Different reactions may be experienced if the G-spot is touched; these extend from sexual excitement to the need to urinate, and sometimes the release of a special fluid which is neither a lubricant nor urine. The illustrations on page 15 show how a man can direct his penis to an already identified G-spot to achieve the best effects. How the clitoris, another arousal area, is stimulated will also be explained.

A man may have a so-called G-spot too, and he may also have both a penile orgasm and a 'perineal orgasm'. The man's G-spot is situated in the area between the anus and the scrotum (see page 19), but can also be stimulated from the front wall of the anal canal. For some men this is the only source of orgasm, but this is exceptional.

A minority of women may have their G-spot

situated in an area similar to that of men. If this is the case, stimulation and lovemaking should be adapted accordingly. Only by experimenta-tion will a couple discover where each other's G-spot is situated, and what pleases them most together.

Position 1

Position 8

Position 9

Stimulation

EROGENOUS ZONES

Before dealing with the five phases of lovemaking, it is appropriate to discuss the external and internal areas of our bodies that are sensitive to stimulation.

The erogenous zones can best be described as those areas on the human body which, when stimulated by caresses, kisses or massages of differing intensities, lead us to feel pleasure and hence sexual arousal. The erogenous zone areas are not exactly the same for males and females, and a description of each is given further on.

For the erogenous zones to be aroused, rather than just irritated, it is normally important to make sure the conditions surrounding foreplay are right. For women, especially, it is difficult to achieve a satisfying stimulation of the erogenous zones unless the atmosphere is loving and relaxed. Nobody can expect to go directly from a stressful everyday situation to successful stimulation of the erogenous zones without due preparation.

A period of relaxed and sometimes lengthy foreplay is therefore normally vital as a prelude to the act of love, as many women do not become aroused, or sexually receptive, as quickly as men.

When the stage has been reached at which both partners are aroused, all skin areas become erogenous zones. At this point, it can be a good idea to stimulate new areas of the body and thereby not risk over-stimulation of the already sensitive, or hypersensitive areas.

Because lips have a rich supply of sensitive nerves, kissing is the most common way to sexually arouse each other. By kissing, you are seeking out and stimulating your partner's lips, tongue and mouth using your tongue. This can be especially pleasing, as while you are stimulating your partner, you are also discovering their particular taste and scent.

Another important way to awaken the female libido is to gently kiss and massage her body. You can start by massaging her neck and nape, then move on to her back and shoulders, and end with a deeper massage of her buttocks and thighs.

Many women also receive erotic pleasure by having their toes and the balls of their feet

massaged, but this will require a much firmer technique of massage.

Of course, both partners can take turns to kiss, fondle and massage each other. The purpose is not only arousal, but also the vital matter of making each partner totally relaxed and receptive to the next phase. It is also important to realise that all parts of the body can be stimulated during foreplay. Time and experimentation will reveal those areas which particularly please each partner.

FEMALE

The ear and ear lobe may be touched and kissed to cause excitement.

The hair may be gently brushed back, and the scalp gently massaged.

The hands, especially the fingers, are sensitive.

As already mentioned, most women are responsive to being massaged on the balls of their feet and on the toes.

The breasts are extremely sensitive, and need to be kissed and fondled very gently.

The nipples, in particular, are most sensitive, and often rise and become erect when kissed and touched. A common complaint by women is that men are sometimes too rough with these tender parts of their anatomy.

The inside of the thigh is especially responsive to touch.

The mons, or genital hair area to the front, together with the clitoris, the labia and the area between the vagina and the anus, are extremely sensitive. These should not be touched until a later stage in foreplay has been reached. At this point, a finger may be inserted into the vagina and moved up and down to stimulate both the clitoris and the G-spot.

The neck, especially the nape, and shoulders and armpits are also erogenous zones.

The hollow of the knee is a sensitive area.

The area between the buttocks is sensitive.

The insides of the thighs, the hollows of the knees and the calves are all erogenous zones.

The region of the shoulder blades is susceptible to massage.

The back is very sensitive – especially the sensitive depression running down the spine.

The buttocks also may be deeply massaged and caressed.

The anal canal area is also sensitive in some women, and touching this area can lead to arousal. A finger gently inserted 2 or 3 cm (about 1 inch) into the anus towards the vagina can be greatly stimulating. To some people of either sex this might not be acceptable, but it is mentioned because the anal area is very much an erogenous zone. It is important to understand that the act of

27 ♀

lovemaking has very few taboos, and many couples practise this particular form of stimulation. Only the particular wants and needs of you and your partner will tell you if this is acceptable. But whether you accept it or not, you can be certain that your actions are perfectly normal either way.

MALE

The neck and armpits are very sensitive areas.

Having the hair stroked gives many men pleasure.

The ear and ear lobes are sensitive to being touched, kissed and licked.

The area between the rear of the scrotum and the anus is very susceptible to touch and gentle massage.

The scrotum and testicles are erogenous zones if caressed and fondled gently.

Men's nipples and navels are also very sensitive areas.

The penis is a most sensitive area, but it is best to avoid touching and massaging the glans and shaft too soon if orgasm is some time away. However, towards the end of foreplay the playful teasing of this area by the female, if she is established with her partner and knows all his needs and wants, is very normal.

The area between the buttocks is very erogenous.

The inside of the thighs is sensitive to a gentle touch.

The scalp and neck may be massaged and caressed.

The spine may be gently stroked upwards and downwards.

The buttocks are also very sensitive to touch and deeper massage.

As with women, it is quite normal for a man to be very sensitive around the anal area, and to become aroused by attention there. A finger just inside the anus, pressed forward against the man's prostate area (see page 19), will stimulate the man's G-spot. However, again do only what pleases you both, and do not act for the pleasure of one partner to the aversion of the other.

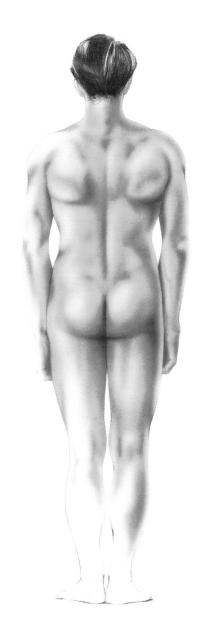

CLITORIS

As the stimulation of the clitoris is an essential part of orgasm for many women, we show the basic principles necessary to achieve primary contact there.

Here the man lies on top of his partner, resting between her parted thighs. Notice how a small change in position enables the man to stimulate her clitoris with the base of his penis.

The clitoris should be regarded as the female equivalent of the male's penis. This means that the front part of the clitoris corresponds to the

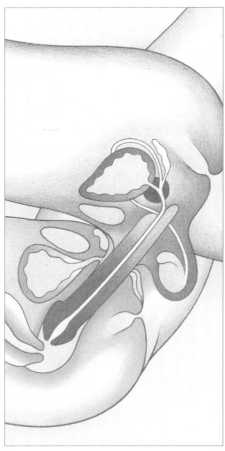

Wrong position

WRONG POSITION

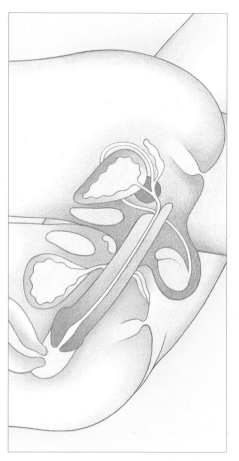

Right position

glans, while the back corresponds to the body of the penis.

It is important to remember that the vagina is not shaped like a cavity, but is more like a slit with the walls touching each other. One must realise that whatever position is used, the penis touches all parts of the vagina.

It should be noted that in the detailed anatomical drawings here and later on, only those parts of the vaginal wall which are stimulated most in each of the different positions are highlighted.

RIGHT POSITION

The Five Phases

FROM FOREPLAY TO RELAXATION

Although scanning techniques have revealed new knowledge about how different positions during lovemaking can affect the interior erogenous zones, it is vital not to forget the equally important preliminary stages.

Exciting and fulfilling lovemaking takes more than just knowing how to treat your partner physically in order for you both to achieve orgasm. Foreplay in sexual togetherness is at least as important and pleasurable as intercourse, and it is essential to remember that the same things are not necessarily as sexually stimulating for the woman as they are for the man; she normally takes much longer to reach the same level of arousal as the man. The considerate and caring man will have to restrain his own needs so that the woman can gradually build up her level of sexual arousal.

The act of making love can be divided into five phases. This is, of course, very much a theoretical division, as the phases merge into each other, one after the other.

The five phases are as follows:

1. Foreplay
2. Sexual stimulation
3. Dilatation (expansion of the upper part of the vagina) and erection
4. Orgasm/climax
5. Relaxation

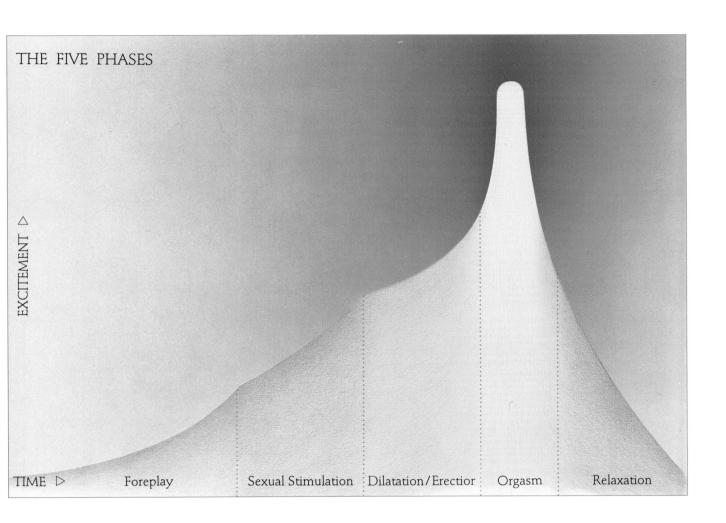

THE FIVE PHASES

EXCITEMENT ▷

TIME ▷   Foreplay   Sexual Stimulation   Dilatation/Erection   Orgasm   Relaxation

PHASE 1. FOREPLAY

As mentioned, time taken in successful and mutually satisfying foreplay is most important. Foreplay is not just the act of stimulating the erogenous zones (detailed in length on pages 24 to 31) carried out before the physical act of love is started. Rather, it is actually a part of the love-making process that ends with sexual release in the form of orgasm for the woman and climax for the man.

Foreplay can take many forms, and each couple will create their own particular and very personal rituals before the actual physical side of foreplay occurs. These can range from secret body language signals to each other, indicating the sexual process is starting, to more open flirting and teasing.

Foreplay for some couples can consist of eating a special meal that starts the longer process of moving towards the sexual act. Many couples obtain great pleasure by whispering and talking to each other about what is going to happen when they actually make love. Love talk about when and where they are going to make love is as much foreplay as the act of physically stimulating each other.

No two couples are exactly alike, and what gives pleasure to one couple in terms of foreplay will not be the same for another. For instance, one couple might delight in undressing each other; another couple might prefer watching each other undress; and for a third couple, the act of undressing may play no part whatsoever in their lovemaking.

Additionally, as couples become more experienced with each other, their particular rituals and signals will continually alter as they discover themselves and find different things that please them, both individually and together.

Basically, however, anything is normal, and the whole practice of foreplay, both mental and physical, is very much part of the entire lovemaking process.

PHASE 2. SEXUAL STIMULATION

Towards the end of the foreplay, when sexual stimulation begins, men and women will feel tension of the muscular system, an increase of blood flow to the genitals, and a sense of warmth in the skin. In addition, the pulse rate increases, blood pressure rises, and breathing gets faster.

The woman's vagina becomes moist, her clitoris becomes enlarged, and the labia swell, especially in women who have given birth. Her breasts become bigger, and the area around the nipples stiffens, as do the nipples themselves. With some women, the face becomes flushed and reddish blotches, which are perfectly normal, appear on the body. The uterus becomes enlarged and moves up backwards, while at the same time the vagina changes shape, becoming narrower around the vaginal entrance and dilating in the upper part.

During this stage, the man's penis becomes enlarged with blood and starts to stiffen, the testicles enlarge and are drawn upward, and the skin of the scrotal sac (scrotum) thickens.

PHASE 3. DILATATION AND ERECTION

As sexual stimulation continues, sexual excitement increases. For both men and women, the skin reddens, and the pulse rate, blood pressure and breathing rate increase. The genitals change colour as the mucus membrane, due to the fullness of blood, becomes dark purple.

In the woman, a sign of orgasm being close is that the clitoris is drawn back and the labia minores become purplish. The lower third of the vagina thickens, creating a cuff, and the uterus raises itself further from its normal position than in the second phase of lovemaking, the sexual stimulation phase (see page 36).

For the man, the head of the penis is moistened with some drops of clear lubricating fluid from the glans. The erection becomes more pronounced, and the testicles increase significantly in size.

At the end of this third phase, the upper part of the vagina dilates like a balloon. This is probably to create a reservoir where the male sperm can be collected, and increases the possibility of sperm continuing up into the uterus to bring about fertilisation in the Fallopian tubes (see page 18).

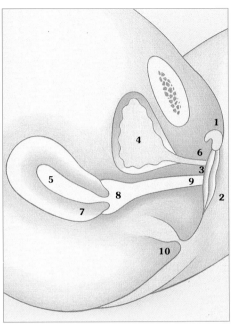

1. *Clitoris head (similar to man's glans)*
2. *Labia majores*
3. *Labia minores*
4. *Urinary bladder*
5. *Uterus*
6. *Urethra*
7. *Cervix*
8. *Vaginal cavity*
9. *Vaginal entrance*
10. *Anus*

PHASE 4. ORGASM AND CLIMAX

For both men and women, the pulse, breathing and blood pressure have reached the highest level. Muscle tension, with twitches in the face, arms and legs, can occur. The orgasm occupies total concentration and nothing else is of interest.

If she has an orgasm, the woman experiences a rhythmic contraction of the lower part of the vagina at a rate of 0.8 contractions per second, while simultaneously the muscles of the pelvic region and anus tighten rhythmically. As they reach orgasm, some women cannot help crying out, moaning or biting their lips. Immediately after orgasm, the contractions of the vaginal and pelvic region cease. Some women, with sufficient stimulation, can achieve more orgasms after a short time, however for some women one orgasm gives more pleasure than several smaller ones.

It must be explained at this point that some women do not achieve orgasm each time they make love, and some never at all. However, many women who never have an orgasm lead happy, fulfilled love lives, and an orgasm is not necessarily an indicator of happiness or fulfilment.

During his climax the man ejaculates sperm, also at an interval of 0.8 contractions per second. Normally, semen is ejaculated in three to seven spurts, sometimes more. Like women, men also experience rhythmic contractions of the pelvic and anal muscles.

As he ejaculates, the male experiences a tremendous feeling of relief and pleasure. During the period immediately prior to ejaculation, this feeling of pleasure will have completely taken him over. After climax, the penis reverts to its normal size. It will usually be an hour or much more before the male is able to climax again, however some teenagers and younger men can become aroused very quickly afterwards.

PHASE 5. RELAXATION

In the final stage, there is a sense of relaxation and satisfaction, and a need for sleep. The pulse, blood pressure and breathing quickly become normal again. The cavity of the uterus sinks towards the upper part of the vagina, where the sperm has collected, and the cervix remains open for approximately half an hour after climax. The relaxation phase is as important as the four phases that precede it. Both partners will have just completed an intense intimate and physical act together. Now is the time to seal the bond together by continuing to gently kiss and caress each other. This phase is often the most pleasurable for the woman – her partner holds and embraces her, displaying total affection at a time when she is most content, relaxed and trusting.

Experience and Feelings

The previous pages contain a short summary of some of the physiological effects of lovemaking. These are things that one can precisely measure and define. It is possible to add a long list of other information of a similar type: for example, that the acidity (pH) of the vagina falls quickly after ejaculation; that the pressure in the uterus, as far as it is known, becomes negative, so that suction of the sperm takes place; that an orgasm lasts five to ten seconds; that foreplay lasts an average twelve minutes, and that the average woman requires eight minutes of intercourse thereafter to achieve orgasm, and so on.

All of this is obviously fascinating, but does not tell us a lot about the psychological aspects of sex. In typical lovemaking, the genitals will have a different appearance, and the pulse rate and blood pressure will increase to different levels. However, this tells us nothing about the very personal experiences involved in making love, which can in no way be put in quantitative terms. It is possible to be very satisfied with a sexual life which is outside the norm, and it is not necessary to live up, or down, to what is reckoned to be ideal by different 'authorities'. Climax and orgasm, and the experience connected with them, are a highly personal matter. Any attempt to give a more detailed description would be highly coloured by the particular experiences of the author, and therefore unrecognisable for many other people. It is important not to allow what others find normal for them to interfere with one's own experiences, which may well be different.

In spite of these considerations, there will still be quite a number of people who, for many different reasons, do not feel entirely happy about their sexual life. For instance, as mentioned, some women rarely, or even never, attain an orgasm when they make love.

It is hoped that this book, and the others that follow in the series, will help such people and, most importantly, their partners as well, to understand more about their bodies and their individual sexual needs so that they can obtain greater fulfilment.

Position 1

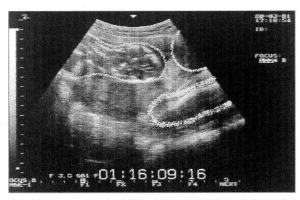

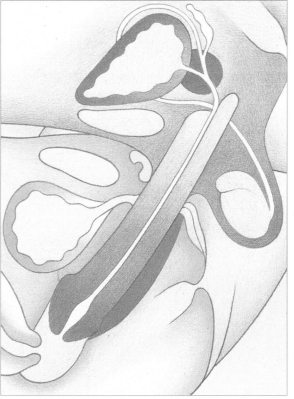

On the following pages, the areas of the vagina which are lightly stimulated during intercourse are indicated in green, and areas most highly stimulated appear in red. The clitoris is shown in yellow.

1. The back wall of the vagina is stimulated most. Optimal G-spot stimulation is normally not achieved.
2. The stimulation of the clitoris is not best in this position either – compare with the drawings on pages 30 and 31.
3. Good stimulation of the glans.
4. The penis comes relatively close to the cervix, which is good if pregnancy is wanted.
5. The hands of the woman are free to caress her partner.
6. Excellent facial contact.

Position 2

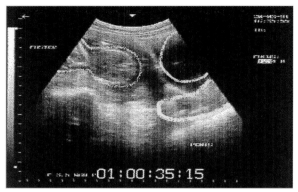

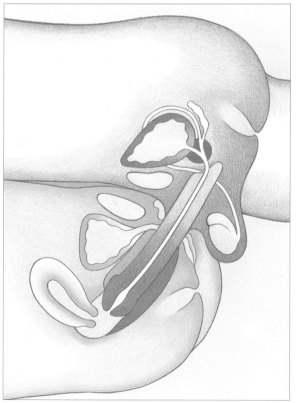

1. Maximum stimulation of the back wall of the vagina, and thus potential stimulation of the G-spot.
2. Stimulation of the clitoris is not always best in this position either. Compare with the drawings on pages 30 and 31.
3. Good stimulation of the glans.
4. The penis can come close to the cervix, which is good if pregnancy is wanted, but not to be recommended during the last half of pregnancy.
5. In the lateral position, the hands are free to caress.
6. Good facial contact.

Many people can achieve climax using this position, especially when it is combined with the variation described on pages 30 and 31.

Position 3

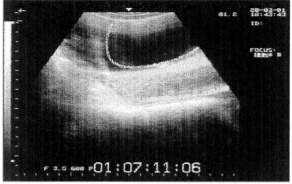

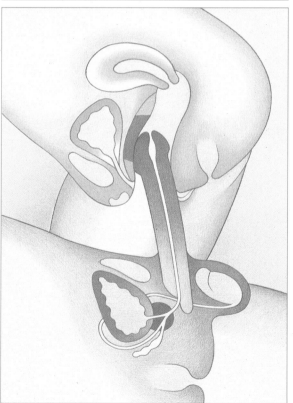

1. In the perpendicular position, the front wall of the vagina, and thus the G-spot, is well stimulated.
2. Normally the stimulation of the clitoris in this position is poor, but the woman may stimulate herself with her hand.
3. Moderate stimulation of the glans. If the man leans away from the woman as much as possible he can squeeze his penis around the rim and thus delay orgasm.
4. The penis does not come very close to the cervix.
5. Both the woman and the man have their hands free for caressing.
6. Excellent facial contact.

This position is suitable during pregnancy or for people with weight problems. Older people can benefit from it too, because it is not very physically demanding.

Position 4

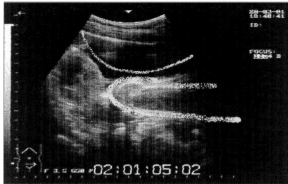

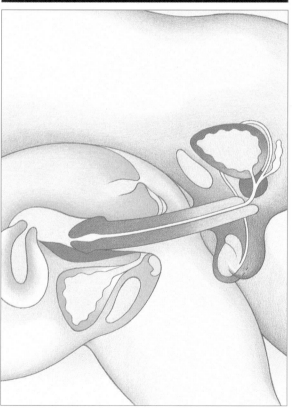

1. The front wall of the vagina receives maximum stimulation, and consequently there is good stimulation of the G-spot.
2. No direct stimulation of the clitoris.
3. Good stimulation of the glans.
4. The penis comes very close to the cervix if the penis is pressing high up into the vagina.
5. Both the woman and the man have their hands free for further caressing and stimulation.
6. No facial contact.

Due to the possibility of close contact between the penis and the cervix, this position is recommended if pregnancy is wanted. While there is no certain knowledge about the significance of this close contact, there is a theory that during orgasm the entrance of the uterus (the cervix) dips towards the dilated upper part of the vagina, where sperm collects after ejaculation.

Position 5

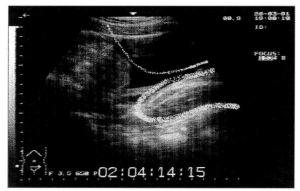

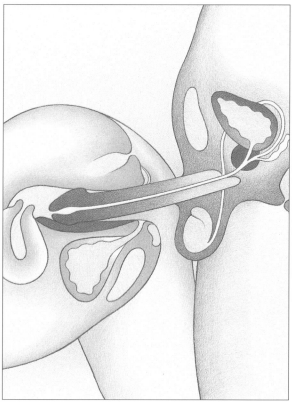

1. The front wall of the vagina is stimulated the most, which gives maximum G-spot stimulation.
2. There is no direct stimulation of the clitoris.
3. There is good stimulation of the glans.
4. The penis comes close to the cervix.
5. The man's hands are free to caress the woman's breasts.
6. No facial contact.

A good position for the stimulation of the G-spot, but also recommended for pregnant women and for those who are overweight.

Position 6

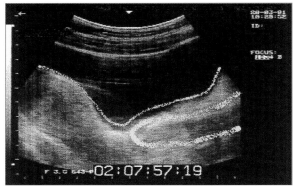

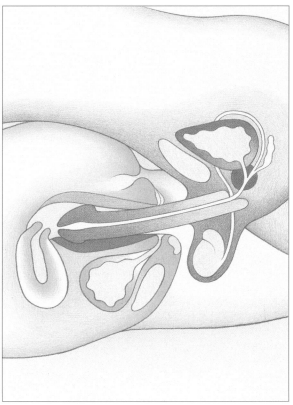

1. The whole vagina is stimulated, but attention is concentrated on the upper part of the front wall, which means there is relatively good stimulation of the G-spot.
2. The clitoris is not directly stimulated.
3. There is maximum stimulation of the glans.
4. The penis is in the closest possible position to the cervix.
5. The man's hands are free to caress the woman's back.
6. No facial contact.

This position is recommended if the man wants fast satisfaction.

Position 7

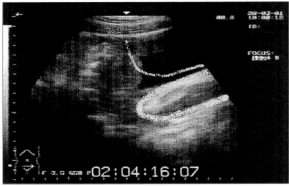

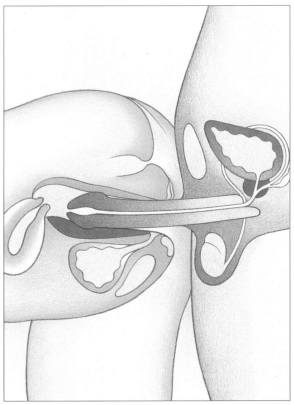

1. The whole vagina is stimulated, but mainly the front wall. The man can vary the stimulation to excite the G-spot to its maximum by not pushing his penis too high into the vagina. (Compare with the diagrams on page 15.)
2. The clitoris is not stimulated directly, but the woman can touch it herself.
3. There is maximum stimulation of the glans.
4. This again is a good position for pregnancy, as the penis is as close as possible to the cervix.
5. Both the woman and the man have their hands free to caress.
6. No facial contact.

A position which many women describe as the best for achieving orgasm.

57

Position 8

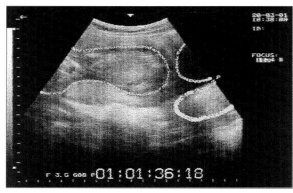

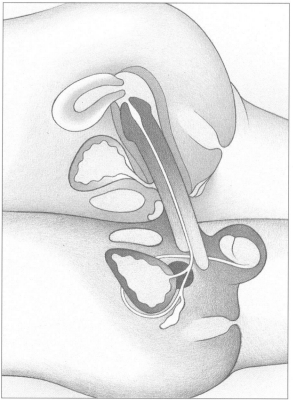

1. The whole vagina is stimulated, but most attention is directed towards the back wall. There is fairly good stimulation of the G-spot, as the woman is capable of directing her movements.
2. The woman can adjust herself to achieve stimulation of the clitoris.
3. There is good stimulation of the glans.
4. The penis can come relatively close to the cervix.
5. The man's hands are free for caressing.
6. Good facial contact.

This position can be recommended to give excellent stimulation for the woman, although it does not always result in orgasm unless the woman has the physique for leaning forward and backward in turn, and moving up and down at the same time.

Position 9

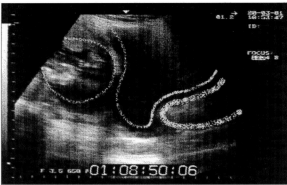

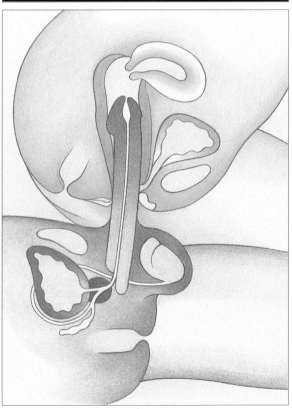

1. The whole vagina is stimulated. The woman can decide which part she wants to receive maximum stimulation.
2. The woman can control the stimulation of the clitoris by leaning forward.
3. There is good stimulation of the glans.
4. The penis can come relatively close to the cervix.
5. The man's hands are free for caressing.
6. No facial contact.

Though this position is not very 'social', it is recommended for pregnant or overweight women. Scanning shows that if the woman leans slightly backwards, the glans will touch the front wall of the vagina, and the bladder will act as a 'water pillow' against the uterus. In this way there will be a water buffer, which will absorb violent bumps during intercourse, between the penis and the foetus. In this position the foetus can be seen resting undisturbed during intercourse, in contrast with the missionary position, where the foetus is exposed to constant violent bumps and shaking.

It is important to note that in most intercourse positions the penis touches or hits the edge of the placenta, which could lead to bleeding and miscarriage. Remember that the pregnant woman's bladder should not be empty during intercourse, as it can act as a buffer for the foetus.

By leaning backwards and forwards, or moving her pelvis from side to side, the woman can vary the stimulation of both vagina and clitoris.

This position is suitable for self-examination.

Position 10

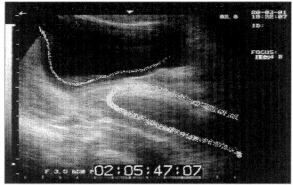

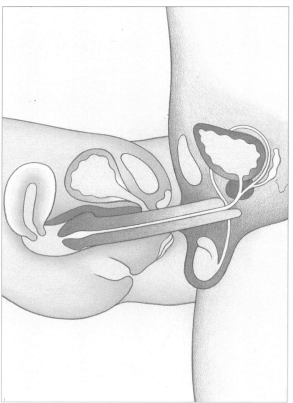

1. This position is best for stimulating the front wall of the vagina, and good contact is made with the G-spot.
2. It is possible to stimulate the clitoris by hand.
3. There is good stimulation of the glans.
4. The penis does not come especially close to the cervix.
5. Both the woman and the man have their hands free for caressing.
6. Good eye contact.

Again, this is a position which can be recommended to those who are pregnant or overweight.

This position may look a little advanced, but that should not discourage anybody from trying it at least once. The position is, in fact, very comfortable, with maximum satisfaction and orgasm for both partners.

63

Summary of Positions

Good ○ Very good ●	POSITION	1	2	3	4	5	6	7	8	9	10
	Page	44	46	48	50	52	54	56	58	60	62
Stimulation of G-spot		○	○	●	●	●	●	●	○	●	●
Stimulation of clitoris		○	○						●	●	
Good stimulation of glans		●	○	○	●	●	●	●	○	○	○
Penis close to cervix (for pregnancy considerations)		○	●		●	●	●	●	○	○	
Hands free for caresses		○	○	●	●	○	○	○	○	○	●
Eye contact		●	●	●					●		●
Particularly good at start of intercourse		●	●	●					●		
Particularly good for woman towards end of intercourse (orgasm)			○	●	●	●	○	●	●	●	●
Particularly good for man towards end of intercourse			○		●	●	●	●			
Good when pregnant (or overweight)				●		○			○	●	●

Comments and Questions

A typical comment from people involved in the development of this book was: "After having had the opportunity to study the changes in anatomy during intercourse, our relationship has become much better. It did not happen from one minute to the next. We had to study the drawings of the scanned pictures very carefully together – of course, interrupted by practical tests now and then!

"Just using our new knowledge we have, in an astonishingly short time, managed to achieve fully satisfying intercourse which is more varied and exciting than it used to be. Furthermore, the 'search for orgasm' is a finished chapter simply because we now know how to affect the points leading to satisfaction for both of us."

One of the voluntary medical student couples taking part in the scanning investigation gave me these small drawings with the following comments:

"Before we took part in *Window on Love* we felt like two separate individuals:

"Little by little we obtained a better knowledge of the function of our bodies during intercourse and gradually we achieved a common starting point, making it possible for us to discuss sex and its many aspects quite openly. We no longer felt separate but had a new, shared knowledge:

"When we finally finished the book we were stimulated to go on talking about sex, but now based on our new knowledge and a new openness in communicating what we felt and thought. Our relationship could now be illustrated in this way:

"The *Window on Love* has become our access to a new form of mutual satisfaction – physically as will as psychologically."

QUESTIONS

Ask yourself the following ten questions. Answer them honestly, and discuss them with your partner when he or she has made his or her reply.

By doing so, you will soon know a lot more about each other. This knowledge may form the basis for some further investigation of the *Window on Love*.

1.	Your favourite position.
2.	Your fantasies during intercourse.
3.	Your favourite pace.
4.	Your most sensitive erogenous zone.
5.	Do you sometimes fancy outside aids – sexy films, sex magazines, massage equipment and so on?
6.	What new elements would you like in your sex life?
7.	How do you want your partner to invite you to have intercourse?
8.	What time of day do you prefer intercourse?
9.	What do you want to introduce into your sex life?
10.	How important is it for you to have an orgasm at every intercourse?

The Author

Lasse Hessel, who is Danish, qualified as a doctor and was for some years a GP in Denmark. In 1972 he started a new career in popularising and explaining many different medical subjects. This started with a well-known medical cartoon syndicated to newspapers and magazines worldwide, with daily readership in excess of 320 million. Many other books, several of them best-sellers, have followed, mainly dealing with diet and especially dietary fibre, on which Dr Hessel is acknowledged as an international expert. He is also the inventor of the unique female condom, called Femidom, launched worldwide in 1991.

This book is the first in a series of six dealing with sexual matters that, via ultrasound scanning and other new medical and scientific techniques, will allow couples to gain a greater knowledge of their bodies during the various phases of love-making, and thus lead them to greater fulfilment.

Dr Hessel was born in 1940, and is married with four children.

Index